AYLESBURY
THEN & NOW
IN COLOUR

KARL VAUGHAN

The History Press

First published in 2012

The History Press
The Mill, Brimscombe Port
Stroud, Gloucestershire, GL5 2QG
www.thehistorypress.co.uk

ISBN 978 0 7524 6623 1

Typesetting and origination by The History Press
Printed in India.

CONTENTS

ACKNOWLEDGEMENTS

With thanks to the Royal Institution of British Architects, English Heritage, Ron Adams, Miss Margaret Sale, the *Bucks Herald*, Richard J. Johnson and Mrs Englefield.

ABOUT THE AUTHOR

Karl Vaughan is Aylesbury born and bred, having grown up in the town in the 1970s and '80s. During that time he became interested in Aylesbury's past and wondered what it all used to look like. In the mid-1980s, during the school summer holidays, he spent time on a few archaeological digs in the town so came face-to-face with the past. In the latter part of the 1990s when he was twenty-five he started his first book, *Aylesbury Past & Present*. Since then he has written a further four books covering different eras of the town's history. He is also a collector of Aylesbury ephemera and runs a Facebook group called 'Aylesbury Remembered' which is becoming more and more popular. In addition to this he writes a regular column in the *Bucks Herald* local newspaper.

INTRODUCTION

We see changes every day of the week but most happen at such a slow pace that they are almost imperceptible – others are so profound that they affect a place for many years. The advent of photography in the mid-nineteenth century enabled us to record these changes in fascinating detail.

There have been many notable periods that have affected the look of Aylesbury. In the 1860s the centre of Market Square was cleared and the clock tower appeared in the following decade. The building of the larger factories in the decades up to and beyond 1900 are represented well in photographs. By the time the 1930s came, Aylesbury had gained a larger population and housing estates were beginning to appear, bringing gradual encroachment onto what was open farmland.

In this book I have endeavoured to be as accurate as possible in showing the comparison between the old and new views. This has led to some challenging tasks, particularly where certain roads have since become dual carriageway or where roundabouts now occupy the original spot. I have used online maps as well as aerial photography to work out exactly where each view was taken from. Once I found the spot I was able to line up the views by looking at rooflines, chimney pots, drain covers – anything that may have existed in the past that is still there today. I am very satisfied with the finished results.

Sourcing old photographs is a lot easier now than it has been in the past. The internet has been extremely useful as I have bought many picture postcards and other ephemera associated with Aylesbury online. One photograph in particular that appears in this book for the first time anywhere is of a building in Walton Road called Walton Grange, which was demolished in the 1940s owing to bomb damage. The photograph dates from the early 1870s and came from the archives of the Royal Institute of British Architects. Sometimes just casually looking for Aylesbury on a search engine can bring up rare and wonderful things such as this.

Karl Vaughan, 2012

KINGSBURY

KINGSBURY IS AN ANCIENT PART OF TOWN as it was once where the lords of Aylesbury lived and also where the old manor house stood. In this view from 1878 are six of the town's many licensed premises. Just visible on the far left is the Eagle, then there is the Cock with the projecting sign, next is the Royal Oak and at the far end of that row is the Black Swan – a Tudor building which was demolished in 1883. On the other side, and almost opposite the Black Swan, is the Angel and the large building on the right is the Red Lion, another ancient inn that dates back to at least the sixteenth century. In the foreground on the right is a water pump which was actually not the only one in the area; in nearby Pebble Lane was another one which survives to this day.

TODAY KINGSBURY IS A TRANQUIL SETTING, rather like it appeared in 1878. In the intervening 130 years, however, there have been many changes. The water pump was replaced by an ornamental fountain that now resides in Vale Park while a First World War tank was sited here for a few years in the 1920s. Then came the bus station which grew in size until it moved to its present location in the late 1960s.

By the time the new millennium came, the whole of the central area was redeveloped and a meandering water feature was installed. Also part of this scheme is a water clock which is just out of view to the right. The large new building on the left was originally built as a mini shopping centre called Kingsbury Court. This lasted for a few years but one by one the businesses started to leave and eventually the place closed. It was given a new lease of life when Bar Med moved into the ground floor and it is now called the Kingsbury. On the opposite side, though, things are rather different as at the time of writing the former Red Lion (known as the Hobgoblin for many years) lies empty and awaits a new occupant.

EXCHANGE STREET

A NEW CORN EXCHANGE OPENED IN 1865 at the rear of Market Square on the site of the original White Hart Hotel. This hotel originally had a private entrance from Walton Street. After the hotel was demolished and the new buildings opened, the lane was extended to the junction of New Road (now the High Street). This lane was given the name of Exchange Street. The old photograph, taken in 1967, shows where the new hotel was rebuilt. The statue is the same one that stood above the door of the original building. There were a few instances over the years when lorries trying to pass almost took it down but it somehow escaped major damage. The tall tree in the middle stood at the bottom of the Recreation Ground. It would soon be cut down because at the time preparations were being made for the road to be widened.

IN RECENT YEARS EXCHANGE STREET HAS UNDERGONE SOME QUITE MAJOR CHANGES.
The modern building on the left is Aylesbury Waterside Theatre which was opened in October
2010. This was built on the site of the *Bucks Herald* and Wilkins Solicitors offices. Also the old
Electricity Board building was demolished to make way for a landscaped area featuring a statue
of Ronnie Barker who went to acting school in Aylesbury in the 1950s.

The White Hart Hotel was demolished in about 1981 to be replaced by 66, The Exchange – a
large office block that occupies the corner of the High Street and Exchange Street. The name of
the White Hart has recently been resurrected by J.D. Wetherspoon when they bought the former
Chicago Rock Café beyond the trees on the right. There is a statue in the new building but it bears
little resemblance to the original.

BICESTER ROAD

BICESTER ROAD 100 YEARS AGO
WAS MOSTLY RESIDENTIAL as many
of the factories had yet to arrive in the
area. This view shows a farmer driving
his sheep out of town after being at the
market. In those days there were farms
nearby so he wouldn't have had far to
go. The house on the left would have
looked across to open countryside – it
must have been a lovely view from
there as one would have seen Hartwell
and Stone in the distance. The houses
stretching up the road were built after
1860, including the Hop Pole Inn
which is about halfway up.

TODAY BICESTER ROAD PRESENTS A RATHER DIFFERENT SCENE with no more sheep being driven down the road – it would be very dangerous to do that as it is one of the busiest thoroughfares in town. Most of the Victorian houses stretching up on the left have survived, including the Hop Pole. Some of the houses have been demolished, though, and replaced by apartments because the land that those houses stood on was quite extensive. The Edwardian house seen on the left in the old view has vanished and another block of apartments now stands on the site. The opposite side of the road has been extensively developed in the last 100 years. The fields have long gone and have been swallowed up by factory units and garages, all the way to Gatehouse Road and beyond. Just recently a large number of the old factories that lined this part of Bicester Road were demolished to make way for a new housing complex called Aylesbury Quarter.

WALTON GRANGE

THIS 1870s PHOTOGRAPH OF WALTON GRANGE IN WALTON ROAD
was taken shortly after work was completed on various parts of the
building. This was overseen by noted London architect George Devey who
was known for his country house style of design. The Rothschild family
used him many times and Devey's designs were used to update and extend
Ascott House in Wing.

   The history of Walton Grange stretches back to the Middle Ages.
The barn on the right certainly shows great age with the large buttress
and timber framing. In 1871 this property was owned by Edward Terry,
brewer and farmer. His family were well known in the town as they ran
Walton Brewery which was a few hundred yards away in Walton Street.
By the end of the nineteenth century Walton Grange had passed into
the ownership of Walter Hazell of the printing firm Hazell, Watson &
Viney. Mr Hazell was known for breeding shorthorn cattle and held the
occasional agricultural show in his extensive grounds.

LIFE AT WALTON GRANGE continued happily until one day in 1940 when something catastrophic happened. On 25 September German planes flew over Aylesbury and one of them dropped a parachute mine which landed right behind the old building in a pile of coal. These types of bombs did more damage than conventional ones because they exploded just above the ground which sent a blast wave in all directions. Much of the rear of the building was severely damaged, as were some houses fronting Walton Pond. A row of cottages on Walton Road were also badly shaken. Sadly the whole place had to be demolished after this event, leaving only the front walls intact. Today the site is occupied by Aylesbury High School and Aylesbury Music Centre.

VALE PARK DRIVE

VALE PARK DRIVE IS A RECENT ADDITION TO THE TOWN and follows the course of the old railway that led from Aylesbury to Cheddington. This line opened in 1839 and the first station was built at the bottom of Station Street and Railway Street. It served the town for fifty years but its site was not ideal because of the lack of space there. In 1889 the original station closed and a new one was built in New Road (now the High Street). This early 1950s view shows a locomotive coming into that station. In the distance on the right are the rear of the houses in Norfolk Terrace.

THE LINE STAYED IN OPERATION UNTIL 1953 when it closed to passengers. After that it was used for the transportation of goods. In the early 1960s the tracks were removed and the station buildings demolished leaving the area as wasteground. Soon after that it was used as a temporary car park. In the early 1990s work began on redeveloping this area and a new road was built to link the High Street with Park Street with some retail units being built either side of it. B&Q were among the first to move in and is the largest retailer along here.

Through the gap under the twin posted sign are the houses that are seen in the old photograph. It's hard to imagine how different this area of the town once was as there is very little trace of the railway ever having been here. However, some remnants of it are visible further down in Stocklake where there are rusting old signal posts and the occasional telegraph pole seen among the trees. The line itself is still visible as a scar across the landscape and is easily spotted from the air as it is almost dead straight all the way to Cheddington.

WALTON STREET

IN ABOUT 1920 most of the buildings on the opposite side of Holy Trinity Church in Walton Street were residential. At various points along the street were passages leading to rows of cottages behind. One entrance, Prospect Place, can just be seen below the lamp in the centre of the photograph. Next to the lamp is one of Aylesbury's many long-lost watering holes, the Ram, which is the light coloured building with the flat roof. Further down, the buildings were beginning to be taken over by businesses owing to its close proximity to town, such as Eborn's garage which survived until the late 1950s.

By the 1930s things were changing in Walton Street. Many of the old cottages were taken down and some police houses were built in the typical late 1930s style with long front and back gardens. By the late 1950s there were only one or two original buildings remaining on the left-hand side. Eventually they were cleared and the road was widened by a few feet. The familiar dual carriageway was completed at the end of the 1960s and the police houses lost a fair amount of their front gardens in the process.

SOME EXTRAORDINARY NEW BUILDINGS BEGAN TO APPEAR IN THE EARLY 1980s on that side of the street. The offices of the Equitable Life Assurance company was the most notable of them which locals call the 'Blue Leanie' because of its slanted design in blue glass. It is one of those buildings that one either loves or hates – Aylesbury has a few buildings like this which divide opinion. A few years later another office block was built next to it. On the opposite side of the road only the two small houses remain from the old view and beyond them are more office blocks and an apartment complex.

PARSON'S FEE

PARSON'S FEE'S NAME GOES BACK TO ABOUT THE THIRTEENTH CENTURY when a few small manors or fees were formed in the town. These included Lord's Fee which belonged to the Lord of the Manor of Aylesbury who also held Castle Fee. There were others too such as Bawd's Fee and Otterer's Fee. Parson's Fee belonged to the church and is the only surviving place name left. It overlooks the churchyard of St Mary's and joins Church Street with Castle Street. The middle row of four cottages were built in the seventeenth century and at the time this photograph was taken in about 1900 they formed a school. Next to them at the top end are almshouses that were given to the town by Thomas Hickman in 1695. According to a plaque on the wall in Church Street they were repaired and made uniform in 1871.

PARSON'S FEE HAS REMAINED LARGELY UNCHANGED although the middle row of cottages have had all their first-floor windows changed from casement to sash and, on the immediate right, a house has replaced the old building. This area really is the most picturesque part of Aylesbury and has a lovely peaceful feel to it. It is a welcome break to walk through here to get away from the noisier parts of the town.

EXCHANGE STREET

HERE IS THE WALTON STREET END OF EXCHANGE STREET, near to the old police station, as it was in 1967. The old wall behind the car on the left is hundreds of years old and would have originally stretched all the way down to Bear Brook. Beyond the wall is the cattle market. That area was created when the old White Hart Hotel was sold off when the Market Company was formed in 1864. The land was formerly the gardens of the hotel. The building on the right is the Eastern Electricity Board showrooms which were opened on 24 April 1931 by the Prime Minister, Ramsay MacDonald. Behind it were electricity-generating works that had been there since 1915, the year when street lighting was brought to the town.

WORK BEGAN ON WIDENING THE STREET in 1968 and new office blocks were built at the Walton Street end which became home to the *Bucks Herald* and Wilkins Solicitors. Originally the ABC Multiplex, the Odeon cinema was opened in 1999 along with the Chicago Rock Café, the Hogshead and Yates's Wine Lodge. On the opposite side of the road in 2007 work started on Aylesbury Waterside Theatre, a multi-million pound structure to replace the Civic Centre. The offices of the *Bucks Herald* and Wilkins Solicitors were demolished to make way for the theatre, as were the old electricity board showrooms a little later so a grassy area could be created in front of the theatre. An amazing survivor of all these changes is the old wall that still stretches from the rear of the old courts in Market Square down to Exchange Street.

FRIARAGE ROAD

FRIARAGE ROAD WAS ORIGINALLY CALLED OXFORD ROAD and on the right is a photograph from 1963 showing the old Hen & Chickens pub. The rubble to the left of the pub was where some cottages once stood and they had been demolished so that White Hill could be widened. Some new houses were built going up the hill and also around into Gatehouse Road. Decades before there was a cottage where the pub car park was, too, and it was picturesque with a neat front garden. The cottage with the green door was at the end of a row of buildings that stretched all the way to the turning for Castle Street. Behind them was Ludds Alley which led from Oxford Road to White Hill. In 1965 the pub was demolished along with all of the cottages on that side of the road up to Castle Street. A temporary bar was installed next to the old pub while a new one was built a bit further back from the old site. Oxford Road itself was then renamed Friarage Road in memory of the old road of that name that originally joined Bourbon Street with Great Western Street. This old road disappeared in 1964 when the construction of Friars Square shopping centre began.

THE HEN & CHICKENS TRADED UNDER ITS ORIGINAL NAME until the 1990s when it was changed to Big Hand Mo's. A few years ago the pub finally closed for good and was boarded-up with some tall fencing being erected around its perimeter. It stayed like this for some time while decisions were made as to what to do with the site. Plans for some flats were proposed but initially they were refused owing to issues concerning the height of the building. There were complaints that it would block the view of St Mary's Church from Oxford Road. Eventually some plans were agreed upon and they were built to a height of three storeys. Something else that has been lost to history is White Hill as it has recently become the continuation of Oxford Road where it goes up the hill to meet Buckingham Street.

TEMPLE STREET

TEMPLE STREET JOINS BOURBON STREET WITH TEMPLE SQUARE and is a quaint old place. Up until about 200 years ago this street was known as Cobblers Row and is believed to have got its present name from the Duke of Buckingham whose family name was Temple Grenville. The early twentieth-century view below shows Thomas Theobald's china and earthenware shop. To the right of it is the lane that leads to the Kings Head. The small shop next to Theobald's belonged to Reginald J. Shelton, bookbinder and bookseller. He also sold picture postcards of the local area. Some of these are much sought after today as they show some remarkable views of the town as it appeared back then. The most prominent building in Temple Street is seen in the centre – the Literary Institute Club, which was opened in 1903 by Lord Rothschild. This family have had quite an influence in the local area with many fine buildings being erected, Waddesdon Manor being the most notable.

TEMPLE STREET HAS RETAINED ITS CHARACTER AND CHARM. The curious old shops have long since gone though, as it is now dominated by estate agents up and down the street. The building that was Theobald's shop has had a facelift as the old brickwork has gone. Further up the street the Literary Institute Club still survives and looks just as grand as it did all those years ago, although it has had its balustrade removed from the roof. It's a shame because it really finished the building off nicely – maybe it was too fragile to keep.

GREEN END

THIS PART OF AYLESBURY WAS DENSELY POPULATED at the time this photograph was taken in about 1900. Many of these cottages in Green End were occupied by farm labourers and builders, some with a wife and several children to support. It may look quaint and idyllic but it must have been very cramped indeed; a lot of these buildings were just two up, two down, so the children would have slept in one room. At least the children would have had somewhere to go and play, though, as there is a big field opposite and Bear Brook at the bottom to go fishing for sticklebacks.

The building below the largest tree was a pub called the Wheatsheaf. In the early nineteenth century there are references to another pub in Green End – the Axe & Saw. It was a popular meeting place and it's likely it was one of the buildings pictured here, though which one it was is anyone's guess.

OVER THE YEARS THESE COTTAGES DISAPPEARED one by one and the field became a temporary car park. In the 1960s the old Wheatsheaf was demolished leaving only a few of the old buildings standing. Friarage Road was constructed (which runs across from left to right) and also an access road for the railway station was added. In 1991 work started on the building of the new Safeway supermarket and its car park. Station Way and Bear Brook had to be diverted and just recently the store became Morrisons.

St Mary's Church still stands proudly behind the trees as it did all those years ago and it appears that some of the trees have survived the ravages of time, too. None of the old cottages in Green End survived to the present day and the last two were demolished in the 1990s.

NEW STREET & CAMBRIDGE STREET JUNCTION

THIS 1947 VIEW OF THE CAMBRIDGE STREET END OF NEW STREET shows how ridiculously narrow it was back then. It's amazing the building on the right stood there that long as by the 1940s the town was becoming increasingly busy with cars and other vehicles trying to get round the place. The building facing onto Cambridge Street is the Nags Head pub. Its history stretches back to the early nineteenth century. Before then it was known as the Dog & Duck. On the left is another pub called the Oddfellows Arms. It too had been there for centuries.

A LOT HAS CHANGED SINCE THE 1940s. The building on the right has long gone. In the early 1990s the Nags Head and its adjacent buildings together with the area called Upper Hundreds behind it were demolished to make way for Upper Hundreds Way, a dual carriageway leading from New Street down to Vale Park Drive. The view was opened up for the first time in centuries and it is possible to see the Chiltern Hills from here now.

The Oddfellows Arms closed around the same time and was taken over by Domino's Pizza. During the conversion of the old building some new lettering was added to the façade in memory of its former use. It may be confusing to people from out of the area who see it for the first time but once they enter the place there is no doubt of the building's function.

TOP OF BUCKINGHAM STREET

THE PHOTOGRAPH ON THE RIGHT DATES FROM ABOUT 1900 and shows an interesting collection of old buildings. The little shop behind the lamp post was a grocers'. We then come to the Rose & Crown pub. At the rear of it was a yard that had stables and a lot of other outbuildings. Some of these were used by coachbuilder George Chamberlin whose sign we can see above the gateway next to the pub. In the 1930s the pub closed and Chamberlin & Sons bought the premises and expanded their business. A forecourt was built to the left of the old pub and some showrooms built back from the roadside. On the opposite side of the street was a large warehouse built by wine merchant Samuel Gulliver in the late Victorian period. His trading was carried out in a couple of former pubs in Kingsbury – the Cock and the Royal Oak.

IN 1979 WORK BEGAN ON BUILDING SAINSBURY'S SUPERMARKET. Chamberlin's site was cleared and it stretched all the way back to New Street. During the excavations some fine fossils were discovered in the bedrock. These were on display in the site office and I can remember going to see them with my school. There were mostly ammonites and they were in amazingly good condition.

Across the road in the 1990s the old warehouse was demolished and a mini shopping centre was created called Kingsbury Court. After just a few years the shops began to disappear and eventually it closed. It was given a new lease of life when its ground floor was converted into a bar. The Bar Med chain was first to occupy it and afterwards it became the Litten Tree. It is now known as the Kingsbury and the rear of the bar looks out onto Buckingham Street.

WALTON POND

THE HAMLET OF WALTON HAS COEXISTED WITH AYLESBURY FOR OVER 1,000 YEARS. It is a Saxon settlement and evidence of those early times have been found at various locations throughout the area. The pond was originally part of a group of at least three in the immediate vicinity. One was by Walton Green and the other, the largest of all, was roughly where the police station is today. This is not to be confused with the present pond in front of that building as that was created in the 1960s when the station was built. The old photograph dates from about 1910 and shows a very clean and clear pond. The reason for there being no vegetation is because it was in constant use by farmers and their cattle. Also horses would drink from it and duck breeding was common in the area. By the 1940s the pond's size had been reduced slightly when Walton Road was resurfaced. Also a pathway with grass verge was put in with cobbles sloping from the path down to the pond's edge.

AYLESBURY TOWN COUNCIL GAVE WALTON POND A MUCH NEEDED CLEANING OUT at the end of 2009. It had for many years become so overgrown that it was sometimes hard to believe it was a pond at all. Mechanical diggers were used to excavate the silt and weeds that had accumulated and it was a very messy and unsightly process. Around the perimeter of the pond some wooden bays were constructed to allow plants to grow on the edges without interfering with the central area. Today the pond is fully matured after its clean out. It's a shame, though, that the plants around its edge have grown so much that the water can't be seen clearly from this viewpoint. The iron railings are the same ones that were in the old photograph while the post on the end has been rather disfigured by an ugly litter bin.

ST MARY'S CHURCH

THE CHURCH'S HISTORY GOES BACK TO THE TWELFTH CENTURY although it was actually built on the site of an even earlier one (there is a Saxon crypt underneath it). As with many churches up and down the country it has been added to at various points in the last 800 years with the spire and clock tower being constructed in the seventeenth century. In the middle of the nineteenth century some major restoration work was carried out under the supervision of the noted Victorian architect Sir George Gilbert Scott. The church at the time was in a very run-down state and was in danger of collapsing. Among the first jobs was to strengthen the foundations of the columns that support the tower. Once this was done work could begin on the rest of the old structure.

The old photograph, taken in about 1870, shows the church almost finished although work on the exterior was yet to begin, and also the crenellated stonework would be taken down and rebuilt in a more ornate style. Among the last jobs was to build railings all around the perimeter of the graveyard and around some tombs. This formalised the setting, making it a much more pleasing sight. They also helped to stop children damaging the headstones.

THE CHURCH STILL STANDS PROUDLY TODAY but like all old buildings, requires attention now and then. For example, in 1976 after some severe gales the Victorian crenellated stonework rebuilt by Scott was damaged beyond repair and had to be taken down for good. When the new millennium arrived some more work was carried out on the building with attention being paid to the clock tower and a shallow wall was built around the top where the old stonework once was. The railings were removed during the Second World War leaving the graveyard open to all.

WALTON STREET

THIS SECOND VIEW OF WALTON STREET IS FROM 1965 and shows a collection of interesting buildings that were between the Ship Inn and Exchange Street. The first building on the right was a café called the Copper Kettle – which can't have been very big inside – and the gap between it and the next building is Bear Brook which flowed under the road. Eaton's hairdresser is to the left of the brook with one of the town's oldest pubs at the time, the Bear. It was a tiny place with low ceilings, carved timber beams and a flagstone floor. To the rear of it was a blacksmith's forge that was connected with the pub's business. Behind the block of white buildings is the old police station which fronts Exchange Street, where a car is just visible waiting to exit into Walton Street. On the opposite side of the street just beyond the post is the entrance to Brook Street which ran alongside Bear Brook almost down to the railway track. It had a row of Victorian houses called Tranquil Terrace which were mostly occupied by workers on the railway.

IN 1967 WORK BEGAN ON THE DEMOLITION OF THE ROW OF BUILDINGS between the Copper Kettle and Exchange Street. The roundabout was put in shortly after when Friarage Road was completed and Exchange Street widened. It may be a sad thing when buildings are lost but it certainly does make a place look different when an area is opened up like this. The old police station can be seen in its entirety now whereas before its architecture was lost behind the old buildings.

Brook Street, which was on the left, has gone completely and now the former Equitable Life office block (Blue Leanie) stands where the row of houses used to be. It is doubtful whether anyone gives any thought to what might have been there before as they drive around the roundabout.

BUCKINGHAM STREET
NEAR KINGSBURY

THE PHOTOGRAPH OPPOSITE WAS TAKEN WHERE BUCKINGHAM STREET MEETS THE EXIT FROM KINGSBURY and shows an interesting scene from 1913 when a group of cyclecar owners stopped in Aylesbury for a rest. Cyclecars were smaller and lighter than regular motorcars and had either three or four wheels. The cyclecars look quite modern compared to the buildings behind them which were very old and were tightly packed together. There was a corner shop there for many years until the mid-1960s when most of the buildings were demolished to make the exit from Kingsbury a little wider for traffic.

THE AREA WAS LEFT AS AN EMPTY SPACE with planters and some cobbling. The rear of the remaining buildings were left in full view for many years until 1998 when work began on smartening up the area. One property in Kingsbury was demolished and some apartments and business premises were built, although they were designed to look old and fit in with the neighbouring properties.

Some interesting discoveries were made during the excavation works; a centuries-old bread oven was found in the basement of one of the former buildings and traces were found of the town's Iron Age ditch that once encircled the hill.

BOURBON STREET

IN 1895 THE PUBLIC BATHS WERE ERECTED ON THE SITE OF AN OLD BREWERY. The baths were given to the town by Baron Ferdinand de Rothschild who gave two-thirds of the money towards the cost of the build. This photograph from 1897 shows what an imposing building it was and inside was just as ornate with shiny, coloured tiles everywhere. To the left of the baths is the town's fire station which remained there until the 1940s. When this one closed it was moved to a new site in Cambridge Street.

By the 1950s the baths had also closed and the place stood empty for a few years. Various ideas were put forward as to what to do with it. Among them was to convert it into an ice rink which was not a bad idea. Unfortunately it wasn't to be as it was demolished in about 1960 leaving a temporary car park in its place.

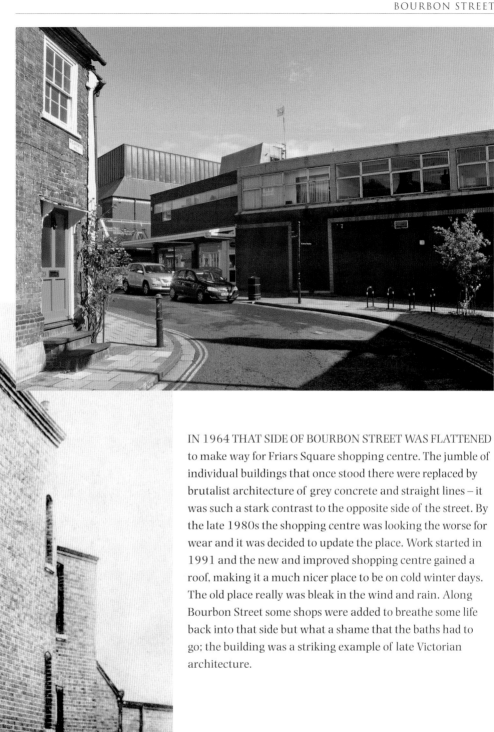

IN 1964 THAT SIDE OF BOURBON STREET WAS FLATTENED to make way for Friars Square shopping centre. The jumble of individual buildings that once stood there were replaced by brutalist architecture of grey concrete and straight lines – it was such a stark contrast to the opposite side of the street. By the late 1980s the shopping centre was looking the worse for wear and it was decided to update the place. Work started in 1991 and the new and improved shopping centre gained a roof, making it a much nicer place to be on cold winter days. The old place really was bleak in the wind and rain. Along Bourbon Street some shops were added to breathe some life back into that side but what a shame that the baths had to go; the building was a striking example of late Victorian architecture.

HIGH STREET

THE PHOTOGRAPH BELOW SHOWS THE FORMER CONGREGATIONAL CHURCH dominating the top end of the High Street in 1980. The story of a place of worship on that site goes back to 1707 when Hale Leys Chapel was built. This was long before the High Street was even thought of and back then the chapel was reached by a path that would have overlooked the beautiful meadows of Hale Leys. The chapel survived until 1874 when the congregation decided they wanted larger premises and so the Congregational Church was built in its place. A Sunday School hall was added in 1895 and extended in 1908. In 1939 the front of the school was leased for commercial purposes.

IN 1980 WORK STARTED ON DEMOLISHING MOST OF THE CHURCH AND THE SUNDAY SCHOOL HALL to make way for Hale Leys shopping centre. Only the tower was saved and incorporated into the new building. It is now used as an entrance to the offices either side of it. The shopping centre was opened on 2 March 1983 by Diana, Princess of Wales who unveiled a plaque which is still there today. The zebra crossing has long gone as the High Street from Britannia Street to Market Square is pedestrianised with access for delivery and emergency vehicles only. Next to the shopping centre the old buildings were demolished and replaced with a bank.

BRITANNIA STREET

BRITANNIA STREET WAS CREATED IN THE LATE 1830s along with Hale Street, Station Street and Railway Street. The New Road (now High Street) which it branches off from, had existed since 1826. All these roads were built on land formerly called the Hale Leys which was a popular place in the summer months. There were meadows stretching down to Walton Road and the view over to the Chiltern Hills would have been a wonderful sight.

Gradually, over the decades that followed, rows of houses began to appear as more people moved into the area. Also the popularity of the nearby railway increased the number of visitors. The corner of High Street and Britannia Street was dominated by a large group of buildings called Tring Villas. They were later hidden by a large shopfront belonging to Longley's the draper and in 1938 the villas and shop were demolished to make way for Marks & Spencer's huge store.

A COUPLE OF YEARS BEFORE MARKS & SPENCER BUILT THEIR
NEW PREMISES IN THE HIGH STREET Aylesbury's largest printing
company, Hazell, Watson & Viney, opened their social club in Britannia
Street. It was designed by Charles Wright in the typical Art Deco style
of the 1930s. Inside there was a dance hall, billiards room, bar and
reading room among other things. Its site stretched all the way back to
Cambridge Street. The club closed on 31 December 1967 and Marks &
Spencer then bought the site, using it as part of their store for a while
until it was eventually demolished. They have since enlarged the store
and now their building dominates that end of the street.

QUARRENDON CHAPEL RUINS

THE RUINS OF THE CHAPEL OF ST PETER lie in fields about 1½ miles north-west of the centre of Aylesbury. The chapel dates back to at least the thirteenth century and had various additions made to it over the centuries. It is the burial place of the Lee family, Sir Henry Lee (b. 1533) being the most notable as he was Knight of the Garter and one of Queen Elizabeth I's champions. It is believed the queen even stayed at Quarrendon for two days in 1592 so the place is of national historical interest.

To the east and west of the ruins are the remains of the medieval village of Quarrendon. They cover a huge area and comprise earthworks of roadways, building platforms and ditches. Also in the vicinity are extensive earthworks associated with a later phase of activity when the whole site was turned over to sheep grazing – this is where the Lee family come in. They built a country house surrounded by a moat with fishponds opposite and a huge earth bank surrounding ornamental gardens. The chapel started to fall into ruin in the early nineteenth century when the Lee family sold the land. Soon it was robbed of its lead and roof timbers, leaving it open to the elements. Many of the tombs were vandalised and internal fittings were stripped. In the 1840s some attempt was made to raise money for its restoration, but not enough was collected and the scheme was abandoned. This sealed the building's fate and within a few years the roof had gone completely and the floor was lifted. By about 1910, when this photograph was taken, all that remained were sections of the arcades and some windows.

TODAY THERE IS NOT MUCH LEFT and no architectural stones are left in situ. Over the years they were carted away and used for repairing farm buildings nearby. Quarrendon is now becoming encroached upon with the building of the Buckingham Park and Berryfields housing estates which skirt round the complex. It is likely that these remaining low walls of the old chapel will suffer more vandalism as the ruins will be easier to get to than they have been in the past. It is well worth a visit, though, as the place has a great sense of history.

HIGH STREET

AFTER THE HIGH STREET (originally New Road) was built in 1826 this end remained free of buildings for decades until one day in the late 1860s when the English Condensed Milk Company bought some land by the canal near Park Street. Two large factory blocks were built and in 1870 the works opened. In the 1890s the company was merged with Nestlé, which necessitated larger premises. One of the original factory blocks was kept while around it some new ones were built which is what we see here in this view of about 1910. To accommodate this expansion Park Street had to be realigned and straightened from the canal bridge to its junction with the High Street. A brick wall was then built around the site to give it that grand finishing touch.

THE SITE REMAINED MOSTLY UNCHANGED until the 1960s when a monstrous new block was built right in the middle. The original factory building which had stood there for ninety years was demolished in the process. In 1994 the chimney was taken down, which was a sad thing to see as it was a local landmark. By 2005 the company had vacated the site and later that year work began on its complete demolition. A developer had bought the site to build some apartments in the style of an old factory. How ironic that they had to demolish some fine historic buildings to achieve this! Only one thing was saved from the old factory and that was the clock which was refurbished and placed on the roof of the new building.

COLDHARBOUR FARM

COLDHARBOUR FARM HAD EXISTED FOR MANY CENTURIES on the outskirts of the town. There was evidence all around of earlier farming as the land near the farmhouse was covered with medieval ridge and furrow. The photograph below, taken in 1995, shows the farm during its last few months before the surrounding area would change forever. In the summer of 1996 an area of land near the Prebendal Farm estate was stripped back so that some archaeological excavations could be done. It was only surveyed for a short time before the mechanical diggers moved in.

Below the ground's surface many features showed up clearly. There were ancient field boundaries and trackways as well as Iron Age remains in the form of circular enclosures. These were probably farmsteads showing that even back then the land was very useful to the local inhabitants.

THE 'MINI VILLAGE' OF FAIRFORD LEYS covers the whole area today and unusually the old farmhouse was saved. Normally when developments like this are built, invariably everything has to be wiped clean beforehand. The old building now sits at the end of Hickman Street which almost follows the same line as the trackway which was there before. The tree on the left looks exactly the same and dotted around the estate are other mature trees, mostly by streams.

The new houses were built to look like traditional ones and some are as small as those old houses once were. It's ironic that years ago tiny houses were being demolished as they were deemed unfit for human habitation yet now Britain is a place where some of the smallest houses are built as the country tries to accommodate more and more people – we seem to have come full circle. At least these new houses have heating and sanitation, unlike their older counterparts.

DUNSHAM LANE

DUNSHAM LANE WAS ONCE A DIRT TRACK leading from Buckingham Road to Dunsham Farm. It was also used for access to the rear of the properties along Buckingham Road. Halfway down the lane in the 1940s a field was converted into Alfred Rose Park, and near the Buckingham Road end Aylesbury Rugby Football Club made Baggetts Field their home. In the 1960s work began on transforming this country lane into part of the Elmhurst housing estate. The view below shows it in progress during the summer of 1966 from its junction with Buckingham Road. Houses on the left side of the road are nearing completion while opposite there is little development. All that is visible on the right are buildings on the site of Elmhurst Middle School and the junior school beyond it.

THE ELMHURST ESTATE was completed soon
after the 1966 photograph was taken. Elmhurst
Junior School has since become the Dunsham Lane
Centre, leaving the other school surviving which is
now just called Elmhurst School. Lansdowne Road,
Caversham Green and Desborough Green were built
on the right-hand side behind where the orange hut
was, while one or two buildings have been added on
the opposite side of the road.

BOURBON STREET

THIS VIEW OF BOURBON STREET from 1964 shows an interesting group of buildings. The white one nearest to the camera was the offices of the *Bucks Advertiser* newspaper. Next to it was a quaint little restaurant called the Tinder Box and the large building adjoining it at the end of the street was wine merchant and grocery store M.T. Cocks.

IN 1964 WORK BEGAN ON CLEARING THE SOUTH SIDE OF THE STREET in preparation for the construction of Friars Square shopping centre. A lot of material was dug away on this side of the site because there was quite a slope down to the Great Western Street area. When all the buildings were gone the street was widened slightly because it was quite narrow at one end. M.T. Cocks' building jutted out quite a way so the remains of its cellars are probably still there under the present road.

After the new shopping centre opened it left most of the south side of the street without any shopfronts, it was just one long wall leading from the entrance right up to Silver Street. This issue was addressed when the plans were being drawn up for the refurbishment in the early 1990s and for the first time in thirty years the south side would have shops again. It certainly made a difference although the contrast between either side is still very stark.

TEMPLE SQUARE IS SITUATED WITHIN A CONSERVATION AREA so
hasn't changed much at all over the years. This view from 1902 shows
a procession through the square of the Hazell, Watson & Viney Printing
Works Band followed by the fire brigade. The whole town would have
been awash with colourful decorations and flags.

The Queen's Head is seen on the corner of George Street and is one
of the town's longest-established pubs. It was owned by the Aylesbury
Brewery Company which took over from Walton Brewery in 1895 –
the brewery had over ninety inns and pubs in and around Aylesbury.
Next to the Queen's Head are a pair of fine Georgian townhouses. The
right-hand one was occupied by cabinetmaker, upholsterer and french
polisher Henry Toovey. He had been in the town for over twenty years.

THE QUEEN'S HEAD HAS RECENTLY HAD A MUCH-NEEDED
MAKEOVER under the watchful eye of English Heritage. Particular
attention was paid to the chimney that rests up against the adjacent
Georgian building. It had to be dismantled and rebuilt using the correct
mix of mortar. It is this kind of attention to detail that safeguards
buildings like these for future generations. Henry Toovey's old place is
now part of the pub and is used as an extension to the dining area. The
exterior has been patched up and painted in a stone colour and looks
very smart.

UPPER HUNDREDS

THIS PART OF AYLESBURY IS VERY ANCIENT – its name's origin going back over 1,000 years. During the reigns of Edward the Elder and Athelstan the shires were divided up into hundreds. A hundred was a guild of 100 freemen, similar to a tithe which comprised just ten. Each hundred had a hundredman in charge of ten tithingmen. They were a kind of police force who had an administrative role and met every four weeks to sort out local issues.

   This view, taken in the 1950s, looks over Cambridge Street below and across to Upper Hundreds and the areas around Station Street and Railway Street. The photograph was taken from the newly built telephone exchange and gives a fascinating view over this old part of town. In the left foreground is St John's Church that faced Cambridge Street. Below and to its right is the rear of the Oddfellows Arms pub with the white building of the Nag's Head opposite it. The buildings then curve around into Upper Hundreds where there was a car park. Beyond this are the old gas works in Railway Street that were next to the Aylesbury–Cheddington railway.

TODAY ALMOST NOTHING IS LEFT of this area. St John's Church was demolished in 1970 and the gas works disappeared at about the same time when Hampden House was built on the corner of the High Street. The next big change happened in the early 1990s when Upper Hundreds Way ploughed through the remaining buildings to join up with Vale Park Drive.

Further changes happened in 1998 when Station Street was deleted from the map as work started on the construction of the Wilkinsons store and neighbouring buildings. It is really hard to imagine all these old buildings ever being there as the area has changed so much over the years.

WHITEHALL STREET

WHITEHALL STREET WAS A CONTINUATION
OF WHITE HILL which joined Oxford Road with
the junction of Buckingham Street, Bicester Road,
Buckingham Road and New Street. The photograph
on the right, taken in 1956, shows how narrow
the street was originally and at the time buses and
lorries had to come through here. In fact there is one
approaching from the Buckingham Street end.

The street once had many buildings opposite the
line of Victorian ones. Up until the mid-1920s there
was an area called Spring Gardens; one of the poorest
parts of town, it was very densely packed with rows of
tiny cottages, all without any sanitation. This rather
belies the place's idyllic name! The building with the
bay window on the left was a bed and breakfast.
A little further up was an open space left when those
old cottages in Spring Gardens were cleared (this
is where buses used to park) while next to that are
some very old cottages which stretched down to
Buckingham Street.

DURING THE LATE 1950s AND '60s work was being done on the Gatehouse industrial estate and inner ring road. Whitehall Street and White Hill were part of this redevelopment and the whole north side was demolished. A new dual carriageway was put in which gave a completely different feel to this once narrow little street. Near the Buckingham Street end some of the cottages on the right side were demolished which created room for a sizeable car park. Something else that has since disappeared is the name of White Hill. It is a shame as it's been called that for a great many years – its modern name now is Oxford Road. Whitehall Street's name is still intact but it doesn't really feel like a street anymore after what has happened to it. Traffic now races past these houses and they are overlooked by office blocks on the opposite side.

THE GRAND UNION CANAL

THE GRAND UNION CANAL has been in the town since 1814. It was originally planned to plough on through Aylesbury and join up with Oxford but of course this never happened. It is similar in that respect to the railway that joined the town with Cheddington as that also stopped at Aylesbury.

This colour photograph from 1961 shows a basin full of boats and some of the early buildings that stood at this end of the canal. The Ship Inn on the right can be seen, which dated back to the canal's beginnings. It was a popular haunt of canalboat people as well as for travellers wishing to stay before they went on their long journeys. Opposite the basin entrance on Walton Street is the garage of Claude Rye, formerly Eborn's. Immediately to its right is Walton Baptist Church.

SINCE 1961 EVERYTHING APART FROM THE CANAL ITSELF HAS GONE – in 1967 Walton Street was widened which meant the demolition of the Baptist church and its neighbouring buildings. In the 1970s some land was reclaimed when the end of the canal was filled in. This enabled an office block called Kingfisher House to be built which dominates the end of the canal today.

In the early 1980s Equitable Life's extraordinary office block was built – local people call it the Blue Leanie for obvious reasons. In 2008 there was a very sad occurrence when the decision was made to demolish the Ship Inn and the former bakery next to it. The council said it had no historic value which is strange given that it had been there for almost 200 years. They were worried that it would look like a carbuncle in relation to the nearby theatre. Four years have passed and the site lies empty which is such a waste; the old pub could have easily catered for theatregoers, all it needed was a bit of refurbishment. The basin now has no original buildings standing, which has left it looking rather barren. Plans are afoot to transform the area, though, but they have been progressing slowly.

TRING ROAD

AN ADVERTISEMENT APPEARED IN A LONDON NEWSPAPER announcing a disused silk mill for sale in California, Aylesbury, in the latter part of 1866. This caught the eye of Walter Hazell who was partners with printer George Watson of London. They were looking to expand their business into the countryside where working conditions would be better. In 1867 the firm became known as Watson & Hazell and they bought the old mill and set up their first printing works there.

Ten years later and with a new partner, J. Elliott Viney, on board they were beginning to realise they needed more room and so they decided to take a bold move and build their own premises. A site on the corner of Tring Road and Walton Road was bought and construction of the largest printing works in the country at that time began. This is when Hazell, Watson & Viney started to have a major effect on the town as many local people were being drawn to the firm.

IN 1885 A NEW BLOCK WAS BUILT fronting Tring Road, and then the single-storey machine hall was added in 1895 although this later had three floors added. When the land on that side of Tring Road was used up the firm bought a huge area on the opposite side by Park Street and began to build there too. Hazell's, as it is always locally known, was a way of life for many of its employees. The firm looked after them and even built homes for some of them.

This fine building seen to the left in 1924 was demolished in 1984 after Robert Maxwell had bought the company and named it the British Printing and Communications Corporation (BPCC). In 1996 the factory closed and the site by Park Street was sold to Tesco which built a supermarket there. The site of the first factory on Tring Road is now occupied by three large units.

OVER THE RAILWAY STATION

THIS VIEW, LOOKING SOUTH-WEST, OF THE RAILWAY STATION AND BEYOND was taken from the newly built multi-storey car park in the late 1960s. Aylesbury College and Sir Henry Floyd School are seen in the distance to the right with the Southcourt estate on the left. The ground immediately behind the station was soon to be occupied by the Schwarzkopf factory which remained there until a few years ago.

MUCH HAS CHANGED SINCE THE 1960s. The Schwarzkopf factory has gone and a new apartment complex called Grand Junction has been built on its site. The old footbridge has also gone and has been replaced by the Bourg Walk bridge which gets its name from Aylesbury's recent twinning with French town Bourg-en-Bresse. The bridge is quite an unusual landmark and as with a lot of new architecture it provokes mixed reactions from the locals.

In the distance on the right Aylesbury College has been completely rebuilt and has a striking new building facing Oxford Road. The only thing that appears to have changed very little is the railway station, although it has had some significant modifications made to the inside of the building. Also the trackbed immediately below in the old shot has been replaced by a car park that serves the railway station.

MANDEVILLE ROAD

THIS PHOTOGRAPH FROM ABOUT 1915 shows the extensive factory buildings of the Bifurcated & Tubular Rivet Company. The company began in Warrington in 1892 and arrived in Aylesbury in 1910. When the factory opened it started with twelve heading machines and twenty-four slotting machines working around the clock.

   During the First World War the factory really came into its own supplying essential items such as gas masks, soldiers' boots, tea chests and rivets for vehicle tyre studs. Like the printing works and the milk factory across town, Rivets, as it was always called, employed hundreds of people from the neighbouring district. By the 1950s the factory was employing over 1,000 making them the biggest employers in the town at the time.

THE COMPANY SET UP ANOTHER BUSINESS in the 1960s called Aylesbury Automation Ltd. This new factory focussed on factory automation equipment and the two companies coexisted for many years although eventually they were merged into one. Aylesbury Automation is now located in Stocklake but they no longer manufacture rivets.

The old factory buildings were demolished in 1997 and houses now occupy the site. One of the main roads on the estate is called Whitehead Way which is named after generations of Whiteheads that were employed at Rivets. Although everything has gone from the original site there is one building that still remains, though, and that is Rivets Sports and Social Club. Also the tiny trees that were planted when the site was developed over a century ago have survived and grown very tall.

THE RAILWAY STATION
AND COUNTY HALL

DESIGNED BY COUNTY ARCHITECT FRED POOLEY, County Hall is one of the more controversial buildings in Aylesbury. This photograph shows the building during its construction in 1965. It is built on land that was formerly occupied by Walton Cottage and the Old House in Walton Street. Before the 1960s the town centre still had many of its old streets and buildings but when County Hall started to rise from the ground it was the start of profound changes to the look of Aylesbury. During the next couple of years work would begin on the multi-storey car park in front of it.

TODAY THE EDIFICE STILL STANDS dominating everything around it. Its original white concrete has since degraded to a dull grey colour. It used to be possible to visit the viewing gallery right up at the top of the building but since a pair of Peregrine Falcons started nesting up there it is no longer allowed. The birds are frequently seen above the town and have plenty to feed on as there are lots of pigeons around. Also the roof is home to a lot of communication devices.

Opposite County Hall a multi-storey car park was built that mainly serves Friars Square shopping centre and there is a covered walkway linking the two buildings. The railway station looks much the same although it has lost its old signal-box to the left of the main building. Also the old footbridge that the original photographer was stood on has been replaced by the Bourg Walk bridge which is built a bit higher so it is no longer possible to get the exact same view.

WATERMEAD

THIS 1960s PHOTOGRAPH shows some of the beautiful arable land that surrounds Aylesbury. The fields are intersected by the River Thame that meanders its way through the northern part of the parish. Over on the hills in the distance are houses in the village of Weedon. They have a lovely view of Aylesbury from up there and also the Chiltern Hills a few miles away.

These fields underwent an immense change in the mid-1980s when plans were approved to build an executive mini village that was to be called Watermead. The idea behind the scheme was to have homes with a bit more prestige than the more regular houses that are found on other estates. The village was to have sporting facilities too and a large lake was dug out, the spoil from it being used to build a dry ski slope. In the beginning the lake was popular with jet skis but after a time there were a lot of complaints about the noise and disruption to wildlife so it was stopped.

When excavations for the roundabout on Buckingham Road were started some Roman remains were found. Archaeologists were brought in to salvage what they could before it was gone forever. The finds were mainly pottery and the stains in the ground were interpreted as field boundaries. The village itself has roads named after birds and the pastel-coloured houses are designed in a kind of Georgian style with large arched canopies over the front doors.

WATERMEAD HAS MATURED WELL AFTER NEARLY THIRTY YEARS. The young trees have grown and the lake attracts a vast array of visiting birds. The ski slope, though, has been disused for quite a few years and sits there like an old forgotten burial mound. Around the lake's perimeter is a walkway that is popular with joggers and dog walkers.

GREAT WESTERN STREET

GREAT WESTERN STREET WAS STARTED IN THE 1860s
when it connected the town with a new railway that was built
nearby. Slowly buildings were erected up and down the street,
some of which were houses. This view from the 1960s shows
the Bucks Motor Company which was about halfway down
the street. The building was originally used by horse dealers;
one in particular was Alfred Seaton in the 1890s who was
associated with the George Hotel in Market Square. By the
1930s it had been taken over by Pratt's motor engineers and
in the 1940s it had became the Bucks Motor Company which
is how it stayed until the mid-1960s when the area was
changed completely.

All the buildings in Great Western Street were cleared
when the construction of Friars Square shopping centre
was started. The once-narrow street leading down to the
railway station became a wide tunnel at the upper end
which was rather dark and foreboding. Halfway down a
roundabout was put in and a new road called Station Way
was built between it and the railway station.

WORK STARTED ON THE REFURBISHMENT of Friars Square in 1991. In conjunction with this a new walkway and underpass was built by Friarage Road. In recent years some attempt has been made to brighten up the tunnel by fixing artwork panels to the walls and painting the rest in white. Also, some new lighting has been installed but while it does look a lot better, it is still nothing compared to how the street used to look in the old days.

Another thing that has changed is the roundabout which has since gone. A new junction has been installed where Great Western Street now meets Station Boulevard and the Bourg Walk bridge. One almost insignificant survivor though is the drain cover seen at the bottom of the old view. It's details like this that help greatly when trying to line things up to take a present photograph.

BUCKINGHAM ROAD

WHEN THIS PHOTOGRAPH OF BUCKINGHAM ROAD WAS TAKEN in the 1930s the Horse & Jockey was the last building you would pass as you left Aylesbury to go north. Before Victorian times it was very isolated as there were no houses in the town direction until the top of the hill was reached. The building is very old and has some low ceilings and probably dates from the seventeenth century. In the distance is Holman's Bridge where, in the field beyond it on the left, the Battle of Aylesbury was reputedly fought on 1 November 1642 during the English Civil War.

In the latter half of the nineteenth century houses began to line Buckingham Road on the east side all the way down the hill. Then in the 1930s some more were built on the pub's side, a short distance from it. In the 1950s Weedon Road was begun and in the following decade the Elmhurst and Quarrendon estates were completed.

THE HORSE & JOCKEY no longer enjoys an isolated situation, nor is it the last pub in Aylesbury on the northern side – the Watermead mini village further down the road on the right of Holman's Bridge was built in the 1980s and that has its own pub. At the Watermead turning is a junction that also leads to a new housing estate on the left called Buckingham Park. It is partly built in the field where the 1642 battle took place. The main road through the estate is called Prince Rupert Drive which is in memory of the event.

The pub itself looks rather unchanged but out of view are a number of extensions to the main building. The largest is a hotel block at the rear which is part of the Premier Inn chain. It is a good survivor in times where pubs are closing up and down the country at an alarming rate and it would be a great shame to lose this old place.

STOKE ROAD

THE PHOTOGRAPH ON THE RIGHT shows a very quiet Stoke Road in about 1910. Most of the houses were built during Aylesbury's expansion in the late nineteenth century. At the time these would have been on the edge of town. The first building we come to was a bakery and confectionery shop run by Albert Burch. He moved to Aylesbury in about 1902 from Hanwell in Middlesex where he previously had a shop. His shop on Stoke Road was newly built, together with Rustic Villa next door which has the date of 1901 carved next to the top right-hand window. Opposite here is the entrance to Old Stoke Road which goes over the railway bridge and in those days into open countryside. In the distance are houses surrounding Walton Green.

IT IS SURPRISING HOW LITTLE HAS CHANGED in the last 100 years. The view looks much the same although some things have altered. Burch's old shop has since become a house and has had its shopfront replaced by a bay window. To the left of it another house has been built, probably soon after the old photograph was taken. One thing that has changed a great deal is the amount of traffic on this road. It is one of the busiest with traffic coming from the Stoke Mandeville direction down to the Walton gyratory system that was completed in 1969. This obliterated much of Walton Green and Walton Place to meet up with Walton Street. The turning for Old Stoke Road still remains on the left and now leads to the Southcourt housing estate. So much of the countryside that existed in 1910 has now been built on and it takes quite a while to reach open country.

AYLESBURY WATERSIDE THEATRE

THIS VIEW OF THE WALTON STREET, EXCHANGE STREET AND FRIARAGE ROAD JUNCTION was taken in 2005 from the multi-storey car park. It shows a few buildings that would soon disappear from the town centre; at the back is the large factory block at the Nestlé site and in front of it are the offices of the *Bucks Herald* newspaper with some solicitor's offices next to it. Demolition work started on these two buildings in May 2006 to prepare the ground for the building of the new theatre. For a year the site was a temporary car park and on 24 May 2007 the first sod was cut by Councillor Sue Polhill from Aylesbury Vale District Council in a ceremony to mark the beginning of the construction.

The 1,200-seat theatre was designed by Norman Bragg of London architects RHWL. Its design was inspired by the Chiltern Hills and surrounding countryside – hence the vertical wooden supports and curving roof. Confusingly, though, the surrounding walls were finished in Cotswold stone which is not often found around the Aylesbury Vale; Wychert (clay mixed with straw) or flint would have been more fitting as they are the local styles.

THE OPENING CEREMONY WAS HELD ON 12 October 2010 and Cilla Black was there to cut the ribbon. Since then it has been the venue for many different shows ranging from *Dick Whittington* to Monty Python's *Spamalot*. The theatre cost an estimated £47 million and has been in the spotlight a couple of times over problems with the signage becoming dislodged. When this photograph was taken in February 2012 an 'A' was missing and had been for some weeks. It's a shame such a building has become a bit of a laughing stock after so much time and money has been spent on it.

CASTLE STREET

CASTLE STREET IS ONE OF THE OLDEST THOROUGHFARES in Aylesbury. As its name suggests, the town once had a castle although there is no trace of it today. It is likely to have been a wooden structure and therefore would leave no building remains. Traces have been found, though, of an Iron Age ditch which surrounded the hilltop over 2,000 years ago. This 1911 view looks down the street from its junction with Parson's Fee. In those days Castle Street was peppered with a few pubs, mostly at the bottom end of the street. The double-fronted white building in the middle is the Half Moon which was an inn for many years. A couple of doors down by Bailey's Court is the Plume of Feathers which was a good deal smaller than the Half Moon. Right at the bottom of the street facing Oxford Road is the Rising Sun. On the other side of Castle Street at the bottom was another public house called the White Lion. The reason why there were so many pubs in the street is because it was once the main way into town from the Oxford direction. There would have been scores of people travelling up here and also farmers with their livestock going to market so they would surely have welcomed a drop of ale on the way.

PARSON'S
FEE

AT FIRST GLANCE IT APPEARS NOT MUCH HAS CHANGED in Castle Street but after closer inspection quite a lot has. For one thing all the pubs have closed, two of them having been demolished (namely the Plume of Feathers and the Rising Sun). This took place in the 1960s when Friarage Road was constructed by the street's entrance at the bottom of the hill. The names of the pubs live on, though, as the cottages there are now called The Old Half Moon and White Lion Cottage.

Something else that has changed is the view in the distance where Mill Way is. The fields have since been built on and the edge of town is now a mile away.

THE RISING SUN
IN OXFORD ROAD

THIS INN WAS BUILT IN THE SEVENTEENTH CENTURY and sited in a prime spot for trade. It stood at the bottom of Castle Street which was the main route into town in those days so farmers and tradesmen would have used the inn a lot. In old photographs there was a water trough by the entrance, but this view of 1963 shows the inn near the end of its life. That decade was seeing many changes in the town and unfortunately for the old inn it was right in the line of where a dual carriageway was to be constructed.

THIS NEW ROAD WAS NAMED FRIARAGE ROAD and joins Oxford Road (its old name) with Walton Street and Exchange Street. The buildings on the right have survived (apart from Matozza's bakery which closed and was then demolished) and for the inhabitants in the 1960s it would have been a huge change to get used to as that part of the road used to be one-way only and accessed from Rickfords Hill. Friarage Road has had a few minor alterations since it was completed. There used to be a central reservation but in the last few years the road has been resurfaced and new crossing points have been installed at the Oxford Road end (this is how it was possible to stand in the road to take the current photograph as the lights behind were on red). As part of a wider scheme in the town bus lanes and cycle ways have been laid out which helps to ease the flow of traffic a little. The bus stops have been brought up to date too as they now have information displaying current bus times.

FRIARAGE PASSAGE

JOINING BOURBON STREET WITH THE PRESENT FRIARAGE ROAD this passage has existed for a great many years. It was formed in about 1386 when James Boteler, 3rd Earl of Ormonde established a Franciscan friarage in the town. It would have sat somewhere in the vicinity of the passage as there are remains of one of the friary buildings at the base of a building called The Friarage which the man in this photograph from the 1950s is walking past.

As for the rest of the friarage site it was mostly destroyed when it was surrendered in October 1538 during Henry VIII's Dissolution of the Monasteries. In 1540 what was left of the site was granted to Sir John Baldwin. A century later during the reign of Charles I it was in the occupation of Sir John Pakington who was MP for Aylesbury and also a Royalist. This put him on the wrong side during the Civil War of the 1640s and when the Parliamentary forces were garrisoned in Aylesbury they damaged it so severely that it had to be demolished.

It is now impossible to know for sure where all the friarage buildings were located as no maps or plans of them exist. From time to time some pieces of evidence turn up. In early Victorian times some foundations were found in Rickford's Hill along with some steps and dressed stone from a window.

THE ORIGINAL COURSE OF FRIARAGE PASSAGE went as far as the footbridge at California. During the town centre's modernisation of the 1960s it was shortened greatly and today it stops at its junction with Friarage Road. It is a pity the passage doesn't look as picturesque as it once did as Friars Square shopping centre now looms over one side of it and the old buildings that were at the top have long gone. The Friarage, however, still remains much the same and is presently occupied by Parrott & Coales, Aylesbury's oldest firm of solicitors.

MARKET SQUARE

THIS PHOTOGRAPH FROM ABOUT 1860 shows a very different Market Square to the one today. For centuries the centre had been cluttered with buildings, the newest one being the Market House in the upper half of the square. It was built in about 1809 when the original one was demolished. Formerly there had been a timber-framed building on the same site dating back to Tudor times. The new building was octagonal in form and had a small bell tower on its roof and later in its life a clock was installed.

In 1866, after a Market Company was set up, the whole of the central block was cleared away to leave an empty area. A new Market House was built at the rear of the new town hall and Corn Exchange. This event also left the square without a clock. Ten years passed with the square looking empty and the locals were repeatedly asking for their town clock back. Eventually a public subscription was held and the familiar clock tower appeared. The main structure was built during 1876 and the clock itself was added in the following year.

SINCE 1876 MARKET SQUARE has retained the same layout with the clock tower being the main focal point. It has been photographed many times over the years and has witnessed a lot of changes. Around the perimeter of the square many of the buildings have been replaced. One survivor, though, is the Green Man pub seen here on the right with its distinctive iron balcony railings. The building next to it was constructed in the 1860s and is a fine example of Victorian architecture. Further up the square, however, the buildings become more bland as they were built in the 1960s. At the top is Lloyd's TSB bank which still looks much the same as it did in the 1860s. The large building next to it though, the George Hotel, has long since gone. It was demolished in 1935 and replaced with Burton's menswear shop. The new building is in the Art Deco style which was popular at the time.

Although Market Square is no longer cluttered with buildings in the middle it does have a lot of trees blocking views of the clock tower. This is a great shame as it looks as good as it ever did on a fine sunny day. The tree blocking it in the present view is almost as tall as it and you could easily not notice the tower being there at all.

CHURCH STREET

CHURCH STREET WAS FOR MANY YEARS Aylesbury's most affluent area as it has attracted solicitors, doctors, surgeons and schoolmasters. Among the most notable inhabitants of the street was Robert Gibbs who lived down on the left in a building called The Chantry. He was an auctioneer, newspaper proprietor and local historian. He is well known for writing a few books about the town, in particular his *A History of Aylesbury* which was published in 1885. On the opposite side of the street are some of the finest buildings in the town. The one with the portico entrance is Ceely House which is named after Robert Ceely who was a general practioner in the latter part of the nineteenth century. He was from London originally and only lived in this building for a short time. Immediately adjacent to its left is the former grammar school which was in that building until 1907 when it moved to new premises in Walton Road.

In 1908 the Buckinghamshire County Museum moved from 6 Church Street into the old grammar school building. In 1944 it expanded into Ceely House next door.

TODAY THE STREET LOOKS AS GRAND AS IT EVER DID and is a lovely place to go to get away from the noise of the areas around Market Square. The museum is still there and has increased in size as it now occupies all three buildings in the row. At the rear is the Roald Dahl Children's Gallery, which is a popular attraction. Also displayed in a glass box is one of the few remaining examples of Aylesbury's Cubitt cars, which was acquired a few years ago and is in fine condition.

Church Street has managed to survive the many redevelopments that have occurred throughout the town. This is largely due to it being in a protected zone. How fortunate we are to have these beautiful old buildings, let's hope they remain protected and looked after so future generations can enjoy them too.

MARKET SQUARE
AND HIGH STREET

IN 1826 THE NEW ROAD WAS BUILT between Tring
Road and Market Square. It was mostly built on virgin
ground until it reached the area behind the Crown
Inn, an ancient structure with a central gateway and
extensive grounds to the rear of it – there was even a
bowling green! Sadly most of the old place had to be
demolished to allow the road to open out into Market
Square – all that remained was the timber-framed
building that stood at the right side of the gateway
entrance. A new building was constructed against it
giving the place a modern feel.

    In 1895 New Road was renamed to the High
Street as it was felt that it wasn't new anymore.
The Crown survived in its altered state until the
late 1930s when it was completely demolished
and replaced by shops and offices. The license was
transferred to a building at the rear of the old place
and was called the Crown Tavern.

IN THE EARLY 1980s the name all but disappeared when Hale Leys shopping centre was built on the Crown Tavern's site. When the centre opened a new pub was established right next to where the old hotel stood; it was called the Bull & Crown. That closed after a few years, however, finally putting the name to rest.

Further changes happened in High Street in the early 1990s when the John Hampden statue was moved from its original site next to the war memorial to its present position opposite the Round House. Also, at the same time the upper part of the street and Market Square was pedestrianised and trees were planted that now partly obscure this view. Today this area is used for community events and is also where the square's Christmas tree is sited every year.

FRIARS SQUARE SHOPPING CENTRE

THE SHOPPING CENTRE was the brainchild of London architect Bernard Engle. Friars Square's construction started in 1964 when a huge part of the town centre was swept clean. Three years later the first phase opened with one of the more unusual structures being the Cadena café which had a rotating sign on its roof (this later became the Wimpy restaurant). In 1969 the second and final phase of the shopping centre opened which consisted mainly of the massive Woolworths store on three floors and the new bus station which had moved from its original site in Kingsbury.

This photograph from the mid-1970s shows the market bustling with people; it was quite compact compared to its original site in Market Square. On non-market days Friars Square was like a playground for kids. They would use the boards from the market stalls and rest them either side of milk crates to make ramps so they could ride over them on their BMX bikes – there was much fun to be had in those days.

THE MARKET WAS HELD IN FRIARS SQUARE until 1987 when it moved back to Market Square, which was nice to see. Four years later work began on the complete refurbishment of the shopping centre; the space where the market was sited was excavated and a new floor put in to bring it up to the same level as the surrounding area. The Wimpy building was demolished bit by bit and eventually a new roof was erected to make Friars Square an indoor shopping centre for the first time in its history – it certainly made a huge difference as the square was normally a bleak place to be in the cold winter months.

The new shopping centre opened in 1993. Gradually shops began to fill the place up but recently more and more units are being left empty. These days people are changing their shopping habits, like using the internet for instance, and Friars Square must face these new challenges and overcome them.

Other titles published by The History Press

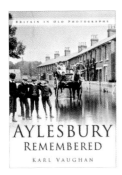

Aylesbury Remembered

KARL VAUGHAN

A varied collection of old photographs of Aylesbury, with an emphasis on the early twentieth century. Many of the images have not been published in book form before. Informative captions and a detailed introduction trace the many changes that Aylesbury has experienced.

978 0 7509 39232

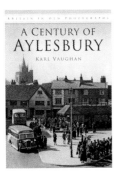

A Century of Aylesbury

KARL VAUGHAN

This fascinating selection of photographs illustrates the extraordinary transformation that has taken place in Aylesbury over the past century. The book offers an insight into the daily lives and living conditions of local people and gives the reader a glimpse of familiar places during a period of unprecedented change.

978 0 7524 5810 6

WANT TO KNOW MORE ABOUT AYLESBURY?

In April 2008 Karl started a Facebook group called Aylesbury Remembered. The group was for anyone interested in Aylesbury's past and for sharing memories and photographs of times gone by. When the group started there were only a handful of members but at Christmas 2009 there was a sudden surge of new members. By the beginning of 2010 it caught the attention of the *Bucks Herald* newspaper which featured a whole page about the group. Over time the group became very cluttered with hundreds of photos all in one album which was not ideal, so Karl decided to create a new page with the same name. The original group was subsequently closed and a lot of the uploaded photos were copied to the new page into specific albums. These new albums are split into different decades as well as some featuring pubs, shops, schools and other subjects. The page went live in September 2011 and since then has grown to over 2,000 members, most of them living in the UK but some are from New Zealand, Australia and the USA. You can visit the page at:

www.facebook.com/aylesburyrem

Visit our website and discover thousands of other History Press books.

www.thehistorypress.co.uk